Outside Hero Academy ...

KW-621-504

Chapter 1: Mr Hench

Mr Trainer was teaching a History of Villainy lesson. "You must learn about villains from the past," he said, "so you know how to defeat villains in the future."

Axel yawned. He'd been out late on a mission to save the baked bean factory. A vat of baked beans had burst and flooded the whole building.

There was a polite knock at the door.

Slink, who had been dozing on top of a cupboard, flicked his tail and opened one eye.

"I'm Mr Hench," said the man at the door. "I'm here to fix one of the computers. I'll only be a minute."

"That's fine," Mr Trainer said. "Come in."

Mr Hench made his way to the back of the room, where the computers were, and unzipped a large, black bag.

Axel immediately heard a high-pitched whine. The air in the room rippled with energy. Then, suddenly, the lights went out.

For a few seconds, everything went silent.

The emergency lighting came on.

"What's going on?" Mr Trainer asked.

When he spoke, Mr Hench's voice was rough. "My power wiper has switched the electricity off. Hero Academy is unprotected. Nobody move!"

Chapter 2: Bubbles!

With a yowl of rage, Slink transformed into Combat Cat. He jumped from the top of the cupboard and launched himself at the villain.

Mr Hench calmly pulled a small remote control out of his pocket and pressed a button. At once, a transparent green bubble appeared around Combat Cat. It held him in mid-air.

Mr Hench pressed a 'down' button on his remote, and the bubble floated to the ground. Combat Cat tried to pierce the bubble with his claws, but nothing happened. It looked like Combat Cat was making plenty of noise, but the bubble seemed to block out all sound.

Then Mr Hench aimed the remote control at Mr Trainer who was instantly trapped in another bubble.

Axel took a deep breath, concentrated hard and became invisible.

Before anyone else could react, Mr Hench swept his arm around the room, pointing the remote at everyone in turn until all the children were trapped inside bubbles … all except Invisiboy, that is.

Invisiboy kept very still and very quiet. He knew that if he made a sound, he'd soon be trapped inside his own bubble.

Invisiboy watched in horror as Mr Hench fiddled with the remote, pointed it through the open door and released a stream of green bubbles into the corridor.

There were shouts all around the academy as other teachers and pupils were trapped by the bubbles. Moments later, the whole building was silent.

Mr Hench lifted his arm and spoke into a microphone in his watch. "Operation Bubble Wrap complete, boss. The cat is with me in Mr Trainer's classroom."

Chapter 3: Too late to run

Mr Hench was obviously acting on someone else's orders. Who was behind this attack and what did they want with Combat Cat? Invisiboy thought about all the villains they'd learnt about in History of Villainy, but he couldn't imagine who it might be.

Invisiboy crept out of the room. Maybe he could stop the villain before they got to the classroom.

A door banged open, and Invisiboy heard the sound of boots tapping along the corridor. He swallowed nervously.

The tap of the boots grew louder and nearer.

Every muscle in Invisiboy's body tensed.

The footsteps were just around the corner. It was too late to run. Who was it?

It was Slink.

Invisiboy relaxed. “He must have escaped from the bubble somehow,” Invisiboy thought. He was just about to become visible and say something when he realised that Slink wasn’t wearing his usual Combat Cat outfit.

Then Invisiboy realised it wasn’t Slink at all! It was Slink’s twin, Hoodwink.

Hoodwink

NUMBER 7 MOST WANTED VILLAIN

Catchphrase: Meoooow!

Hobbies: chasing string, plotting to take over Hero Academy.

Likes: sleeping, eating, catnip.

Dislikes: having his ears cleaned, vets.

Beware! Hoodwink can easily be mistaken for Slink. He was created when Slink was accidentally copied by a duplicating gadget. Hoodwink escaped and has been plotting and scheming ever since.

Invisiboy held his breath as Hoodwink stopped and sniffed the air. Invisiboy was going to be discovered! He'd be trapped in a bubble in seconds!

Just then, Mr Hench called out, "In here, boss."

Hoodwink turned away. Invisiboy tried not to let all his breath out at once.

Hoodwink stopped just outside the classroom. He reached into his pocket and pulled out a small mirror and comb.

Invisiboy couldn't believe his eyes. The villainous cat was combing his whiskers!

Then Hoodwink pulled out a fishbone and used it to clean between his teeth.

Invisiboy grinned. He had an idea!

Chapter 4:
A distraction

As soon as Hoodwink entered the classroom, Invisiboy turned and ran to the kitchen. The one thing that Slink liked more than anything else was fish. Invisiboy just hoped that Slink's twin would be the same ...

Invisiboy burst into the kitchen. In the soft glow of the emergency lights, he raced across the room, towards the fridge. He rummaged through it until he found what he was looking for: a large, raw, silver fish.

Invisiboy grabbed the plate with the fish on and dashed back to the classroom.

As Invisiboy approached the classroom, he heard Mr Hench's gruff voice. "That's right, boss. Now that Combat Cat and all the other heroes are captured, the Head will have no choice but to surrender Hero Academy to you."

Very quietly, Invisiboy tiptoed into the room.

Hoodwink was meowing loudly, and Mr Hench was nodding.

"Yeah!" Mr Hench agreed. "You're in charge now, Headmaster Hoodwink."

Neither of them noticed as Invisiboy placed the fish on a table.

"Like you said," Mr Hench continued, "you could run this place better than the Head." He paused. "Um … boss?"

Hoodwink had spotted the fish. He jumped up on to a chair and was looking greedily at the fish.

Mr Hench cleared his throat. “Boss, I don’t think that’s a good idea. We don’t know ...”

Invisiboy had to stop himself from laughing as Hoodwink sank his fangs into the fish.

“Er, boss?” said Mr Hench. “Boss?”

Chapter 5: Time to leave

Invisiboy was just wondering what to do next when he noticed Mr Hench's shoelaces were undone.

While Hoodwink chewed his way through the tastiest fish he'd eaten in years, Invisiboy crouched down in front of Mr Hench.

Carefully, Invisiboy grasped a loose lace from each shoe. He tied them together, then stood up and suddenly made himself visible again.

Mr Hench yelped in surprise and fell backwards. He dropped the remote control, which skidded across the floor.

Axel picked it up and pointed it straight at Hoodwink.

“BOSS!” Mr Hench yelled, while struggling to untie his shoelaces.

Hoodwink took the last bite of his fish, then he looked up.

Before the cat could move, Axel pressed a button on the remote control. Hoodwink was trapped in a green bubble.

Axel’s classmates silently clapped inside their bubbles as Axel turned the remote on Mr Hench. As quick as a flash, Mr Hench was also surrounded by a bubble.

Axel pressed a couple of buttons on the remote control until he worked out how to remove the bubbles. Then he walked around the room, freeing Combat Cat, Mr Trainer and the rest of the heroes.

Combat Cat curled around Axel's leg, purring. Then he walked over to Hoodwink's bubble, and glared at his twin.

Hoodwink, who was looking slightly unwell after eating the whole fish, scowled back and then coughed up a fishbone.

Mr Trainer turned the power back on, then he said to Axel, “Could you give me a hand, please? I think it’s time we got these two out of here.”

Axel pressed the ‘down’ button on the remote, and Hoodwink’s and Mr Hench’s bubbles floated to the ground.

Axel and Mr Trainer pushed the two bubbles along the corridor and out of Hero Academy.

The second they got outside, Hoodwink leapt to his feet. Then he started to run!

As Hoodwink ran, the bubble started to roll across the grass. It went faster and faster, until Hoodwink was just a blur inside.

Mr Hench took one look at Hoodwink and did the same.

"Should we go after them?" Axel asked.

Mr Trainer shook his head and chuckled. "Don't worry. The Head has sent a message to Police Commissioner Jordan. They won't get far!"